Answers About

The MOON, STARS and PLANETS

Written by
FREDERICK SMITHLINE

Illustrated by
RAUL MINA MORA,
JAMES PONTER, and
DENNY McMAINS

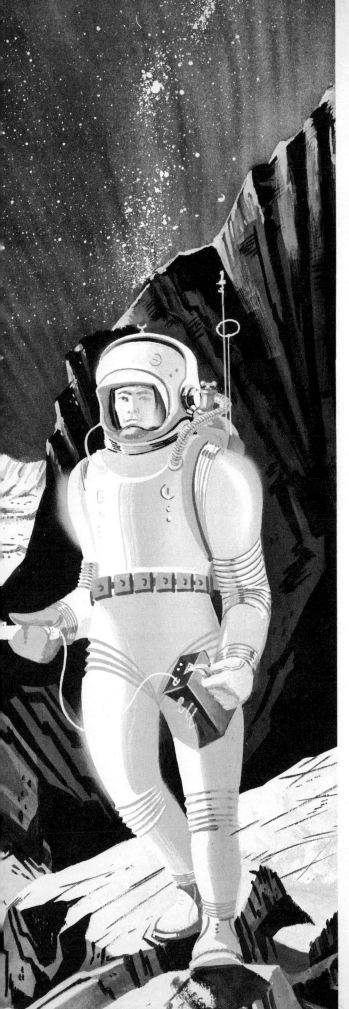

GROSSET & DUNLAP · Publishers
NEW YORK

Library of Congress Catalog Card Number: 76-86700

CONTENTS

WHAT DO WE SEE UP IN THE SKY?

If you look up at the sky on a clear night, what do you see? There are thousands of lights against a dark background. Let's pretend at first that we know nothing but what we can see. Then it will be easy to understand what people first thought about these lights in the sky and how they slowly pieced together the wonderful facts and ideas that make up the science of astronomy.

Let's say that we are standing in a place where there are no buildings or trees or mountains to block our view of the sky, for instance on the deck of a ship in the ocean. The sky will look to us the same as it looked to the earliest man on earth. Beyond our ship all we can see is water and sky. It is as if we were alone in an empty house. The surface of the ocean makes the floor. It appears to be flat and perfectly round. We seem to be exactly in the center of it. The house appears to be covered by a dome.

Looking all around us we can see where the sky and earth seem to meet in a circle. We name this circle the horizon.

As we look up from the horizon in any direction, there are the lights of the stars in the dome of the sky. On some nights the moon appears and the fainter stars fade from view. On dark nights a band of milky light extends across part of the sky. By day the blinding light of the sun is all we can see in the sky.

WHAT DID PRIMITIVE MAN SEE UP IN THE SKY?

This is the way the universe looked to primitive people, and so it is the way they believed it to be. They believed the earth was flat, because it looks flat. They believed the horizon was the edge of the earth, because you can't see anything beyond it. And they believed that the sky was the dome-shaped roof of the world.

When you look at the stars the first thing you notice is that some are brighter than others. Then you notice that some of the bright ones make patterns that are easy to remember. These patterns of the stars are called constellations. The ancient Greeks gave them names and made up myths about them. By naming the constellations, they created a

Despite his awesome fear of the heavens, primitive man began to chart time by the sun's position in the sky and the shape of the moon.

map of the sky. Just as a map of the United States shows that Chicago is in Illinois, the map of the constellations shows that Polaris, the North Star, is in the constellation Ursa Minor, the Little Bear.

As soon as men recognized a pattern of stars as a constellation, they were able to make a great discovery. The stars move. A single constellation can be found in different parts of the sky at different times. But the patterns themselves never change; all the stars seem to move together. It seemed obvious to ancient men that the sky itself moved and all the stars were attached to it. But were they all? As men watched the sky they discovered that a few of the brightest stars did not stay in a particular constellation. At different times of the year they could be seen in different constellations. These lights were called wanderers. From the Greek word for "wanderer" we get our word *planet*.

HOW DO WE LEARN ABOUT SPACE AND WHAT IT CONTAINS?

It was not until some 300 years ago, when the famous Italian astronomer Galileo looked through his telescope and told about the other worlds he saw, that men realized there were other worlds in addition to our earth. They began to dream of reaching these worlds. Man has been probing space ever since he first turned his eyes skyward to observe the sun, moon and stars. While the telescope provided much information about the heavens, it is only recently that we have obtained detailed information about the space surrounding the earth.

We gathered this information in many ways. First, astronomers used the spectroscope (SPEC-tro-scope) with their telescopes to determine the composition of the stars. Radio telescopes have provided us with more information than the large 200-inch telescope at Mount Palomar, California. To use a radio telescope, we send radio signals into space, aiming at some part of the sky. These waves bounce back from any object in the sky, such as the moon or a star, in the same way as a ball bounces back to you when you throw it against a wall. The telescope picks up these waves, and scientists, by studying the time it took the waves for their entire trip, can plot surface maps of the heavenly bodies.

Ever since early history, man has been curious. First, he explored his cave, then the land, next the sea and eventually the air. Today, man stands at a new frontier — space and space travel. As we go up into the air over the earth, we will not find any road sign along the way saying, "You are now entering space." Actually, once we leave the ground we are in space. The airplanes that fly overhead are in space. But they are only at the very bottom of space. Today, man is interested in *outer space*.

Although scientists have not agreed upon where outer space begins, there are many who feel that once we are about 600 miles above the earth, we are at the bottom fringe of outer space. If this is the bottom, where is the top? The top or farthest reaches of outer space is millions and millions of miles away. No matter how far away from the earth we go, we would still be in outer space. In effect, we would be traveling through the universe (U-ni-verse). The universe is the biggest thing we can picture. Everything we know of is in the universe — our earth, the sun, the very distant stars. Therefore, no matter how far out we go from earth, either by exploring with our telescopes or flying in a spaceship, we would always be in the universe and never reach the end of outer space.

WHAT PLANET DO WE KNOW THE MOST ABOUT?

The heavenly body with which we are most familiar is the earth. It is one of the nine major planets that revolve about the sun. A *planet* (PLAN-et) is a heavenly body which revolves about a sun. It shines not because of its own light but by the reflection of light from the sun. For example, if you took a lighted electric bulb, it could resemble our sun. Then if you placed a mirror-surfaced ball near it, you would think that the ball was lighted. Actually, the ball is only reflecting the light from the electric bulb.

In addition to the planets there are perhaps 100,000 *planetoids* (PLAN-et-oids), also called *minor planets* or *asteroids* (AS-ter-oids). They differ from the major planets, such as the earth, mainly in size.

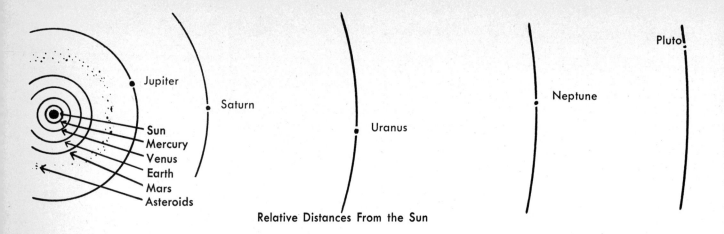

Relative Distances From the Sun

WHICH IS THE NEAREST HEAVENLY BODY TO EARTH?

The next most familiar heavenly body to us is our moon. It is a *satellite* (SAT-el-lite) or a heavenly body that revolves around a larger one in much the same way that the earth is a satellite of the sun. Six of the nine major planets have one or more satellites, or moons, revolving around them. While the earth has only one moon, the planet Jupiter has twelve.

Also revolving around the sun are a number of *comets* (COM-ets). The typical comet has a head and a tail. The head consists of a mixture of gases and small solid particles similar to meteorites. The tail is comprised of many gases. The comet glows as it moves through the heavens. Many of the comets revolve around the sun in the same manner as the planets, while others come from some distance away in the universe, pass around the sun and then disappear.

WHAT IS THE SOLAR SYSTEM?

Together, the major planets, their satellites, the asteroids, comets, meteorites and our sun form the solar system. This solar system, with the billions of stars that surround it, forms our *galaxy* (GAL-ax-y). The galaxy in which we live is called the Milky Way. If we join our galaxy with all the other many billions of galaxies, we then have the universe.

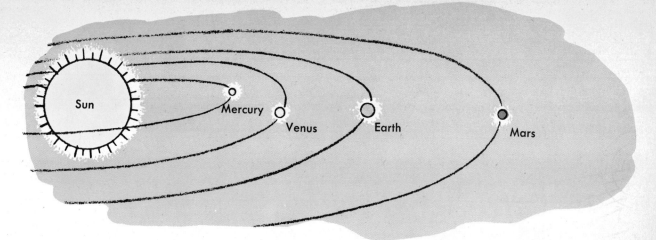

If you were able to stand in space millions of miles above the North Pole and observe our solar system, you would find all the planets circling about the sun in a counterclockwise direction, like the hands of a clock running backwards. Why do the planets follow this pattern? If you take a model airplane tied to a string, and let it fly in a circle around you, you will find that as long as the airplane travels at the same speed, it stays in the same path and it stays the same distance from you. The same is true of the sun and earth even though there is no string between them. As the earth and the other planets travel around the sun, they are pulling away from the sun. However, there is another force that is "pulling" on the earth — that is gravity (GRAV-i-ty). The sun's gravity pulls on the earth and the planets in the same way that the earth's gravity pulls on you. All bodies in the universe have a gravitational attraction on each other.

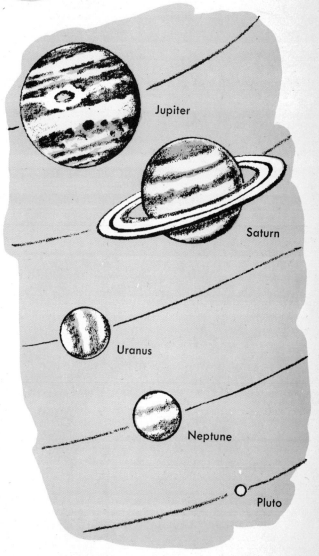

The comparative sizes of the sun and planets and their distances apart cannot be shown in one picture. This is because the sun is so tremendously bigger than the planets, and the distances between the planets are so vast compared with their sizes.

HOW DOES GRAVITY WORK?

If you throw a ball into the air, it falls to earth because of the pull of gravity. In the seventeenth century, Sir Isaac Newton of England discovered what we call the "laws" of gravity. He found that all bodies in the universe have an attraction power, and that the power force of gravity depends upon several things. First, the greater the amount of matter or weight of a body, the greater is its gravity pull. For example, the earth has a greater gravitational pull than the moon, just as the sun has a greater gravitational pull than the earth. Second, Newton found that the distance between the bodies affects the strength of this force. Thus, gravity has a stronger pull when the two bodies are closer together than when they are farther apart.

WHAT MOVEMENTS DO THE PLANETS MAKE?

The planets revolve about the sun in a planetary orbit; that is, they move in an ellipse (e-LIPSE) or elongated circle. To draw an ellipse, stick two thumbtacks into a piece of cardboard about four inches apart.

The earth, like the other planets and asteroids, revolves about the sun in an elliptical orbit. You can draw these orbits of our solar system, using a pencil, two thumbtacks and a piece of string.

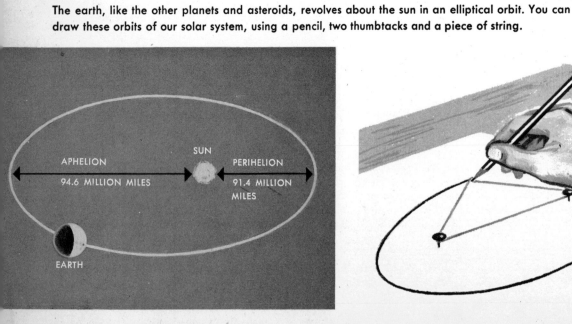

APHELION
94.6 MILLION MILES

SUN

PERIHELION
91.4 MILLION MILES

EARTH

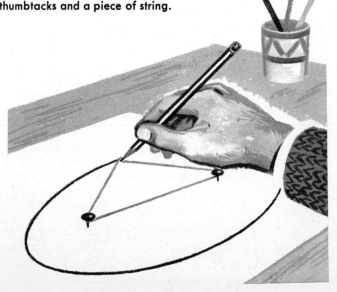

Make a loop of string about four inches long and slip it over the tacks. The loop should not be too taut. Stick a pencil point through the loop and stretch the loop out. Then, holding the pencil in this fashion, move it along the string and draw on the cardboard. You have now drawn an ellipse. The points where the thumbtacks are placed are called the focal points of the ellipse. It was the German astronomer Kepler who proved that the planets revolve about the sun in an elliptical or planetary orbit and that the sun is located at one of the focal points.

The earth, like the other planets, travels about the sun in an elliptical orbit. At its nearest point, or *perihelion* (per-i-HE-li-on), the earth is 91.4 million miles away from the sun. At its farthest point, or *aphelion* (a-PHE-li-on), the earth is 94.6 million miles from the sun. The average distance between the earth and sun, according to astronomers, is 93 million miles.

WHAT MOVEMENTS DOES THE EARTH MAKE?

Did you ever spin a top or a gyroscope? As the top or gyroscope turns round and round rapidly, it is rotating (RO-TAT-ing). Astronomers know that all the planets, including the earth, rotate around their own axis, or an imaginary line drawn through the center of the earth from the North Pole to the South Pole. It is this rotating motion that causes night and day. As the earth spins on its axis, part of it faces the sun and the other part faces away from the sun. One complete rotation takes twenty-four hours or a day. At times, we refer to half a rotation as daytime and the other half as nighttime.

This rotating motion is called *sidereal* (si-DER-al) motion by astronomers. Hold a ball in your hand between the thumb and index finger. At the point where the thumb touches the ball, picture the South Pole, and where the index finger touches the ball, the North Pole. Put a chalk mark halfway between the poles. This will be the equator or middle of the earth. Now place another chalk mark near the North Pole. As you rotate the ball and make one complete turn, you will see that the mark at the equator has to travel a bigger distance than the mark near the pole.

In other words, the mark at the equator has to travel faster than the mark near the pole since it covers a longer distance.

At the same time that the earth is rotating, it is also moving around the sun. This movement is called *revolution* (rev-o-LU-tion). One complete trip around the sun is one revolution, or, as we know it, one year. To make this trip the earth travels at a speed of 18½ miles per second. In one hour it covers more than 66,600 miles in space on its orbital trip around the sun.

The axis of the earth (red arrows) is tilted with reference to the plane of its orbit (yellow band). This causes unequal days and nights over most of the world.

As the earth moves around the sun, one pole or the other is pointed more toward the sun, because the earth's axis is tilted. The slight change in distance from the earth to the sun during the year is not shown, because it has nothing to do with the seasons.

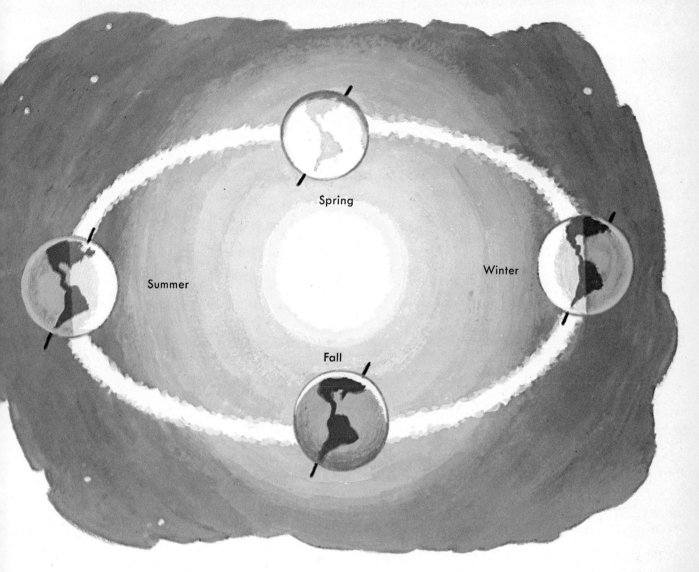

WHAT IS THE ASTEROID BELT?

Between the orbits of the planets Mars and Jupiter is a space some 350 million miles wide. For many years, astronomers thought that there should be a planet in this space because it was so large and it left a gap in what they considered the normal spacing between planets. In 1801, astronomers found a heavenly body only about 480 miles wide. They watched it through their telescopes and found that it revolved around the sun like a planet. Several years later they discovered many more "small planets" in this portion of the sky. Today, we know this region as the asteroid belt. It is believed to include more than 100,000 planetoids or asteroids. Some are ball-shaped, like the earth, while others are like irregular chunks of rock. The largest of the asteroids is Ceres, 480 miles in diameter, or about the width of Texas. Other known asteroids are much smaller. Adonis, Apollo and Hermes are only about a mile or less in diameter.

Between these asteroids and the sun are the *inner planets* — Mercury, Venus, Earth and Mars. The planets beyond the asteroids — Jupiter, Saturn, Uranus, Neptune and Pluto — are known as the *outer planets.*

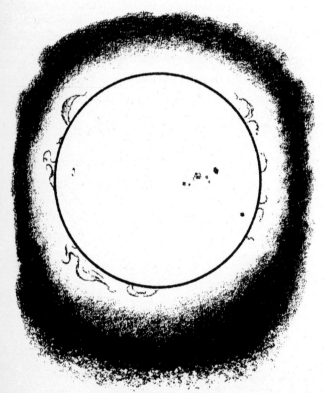

The sunspots shown are huge storms covering areas larger than the earth's diameter. The flares around the edge are great eruptions of fiery gases thousands of miles long.

WHAT SUPPLIES THE
SOLAR SYSTEM'S ENERGY?

Look first at the sun, then at the sun's family of planets, of which our earth is a member. The family is called the solar system, from the Latin word *solus,* for sun. Throughout all the centuries, up until man first released atomic energy in the 1940's, the sun has been earth's only power plant. All the usable energy on earth has come from the sun. When primitive man burned a log of wood, he was releasing energy from the sun's rays stored in the wood by the processes of life in the tree. The energy from the food we eat can be traced to the sun in the same way. Electricity produced by water falling over a dam is energy from the sun because the sun's heat had to raise up the water by evaporation before it could fall back to earth as rain and run down the rivers.

For centuries men wondered how the sun could continue to put out so much heat energy without burning up. The answer we now know is that the sun does not burn. It is an atomic-energy furnace that produces its energy by the same process as the hydrogen bomb. The immediate question that arises is: "Why doesn't the sun blow up like a hydrogen bomb?" And the answer is: because it is so big. Remember, Newton discovered that every particle of matter attracts every other particle. In the sun there are so many atoms that their attraction for each other is strong enough to resist the fantastic forces — greater than those in the hydrogen bomb — that are thrusting atoms apart.

WHAT IS THE SUN LIKE INSIDE?

The sun is more than a million times bigger than the earth. Its diameter is 864,000 miles as compared with the earth's 7,927 miles. But the sun is not nearly a million times heavier than the earth. Its mass is only about 332,000 times as great as the earth's. (The word "only" sounds funny with a figure that, in terms of weight on the surface of the earth, would mean 4,380,000,000,000,000,000,000,000,000,000 pounds.) The sun is all gas. It may be hard to imagine a ball of gas in space. We think of gas as a substance that escapes unless we keep it closed in, like the gas in a toy balloon. But again, it is gravity that holds the gas together in the sun, just as the gravity of the earth holds its layer of air around it. The gravity of the sun is vastly greater than that of the earth. The attraction of the sun's atoms toward its center compresses them so much that a piece from the middle of the sun would be heavier than a block of iron the same size. Yet the center of the sun has not been squeezed into a solid core or even into liquid. It is so hot in the sun that nothing can exist as a solid or liquid.

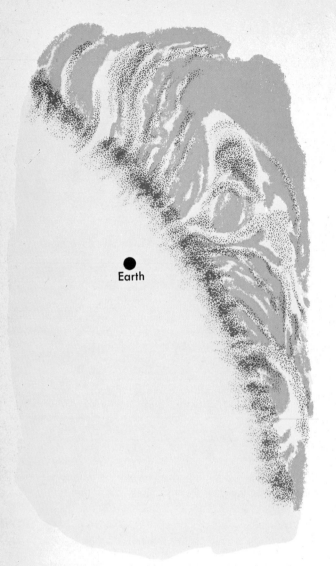

The black spot represents the size of the earth against the surface of the sun.

Earth

The heat at the center of the sun is estimated at about 35,000,000 degrees on the same kind of Fahrenheit scale that the weatherman uses. Outward from the center the temperature grows gradually lower. At the "surface," the face of the sun from which we get our heat, is only 11,000 degrees.

CAN SOME OF THE SUN'S RAYS BE DANGEROUS?

Inside the sun gases are pressed together by pressure. The pressure is so great that the atoms, or basic chemical elements in the helium and hydrogen gases, are crushed together. This crushing together of the atoms results in a tremendous release of energy, which is given off as heat, light and other rays. Cosmic rays are one of these other rays and they travel at a very, very high speed. These rays spread out from the sun in all directions and some reach the earth.

Exposure to a large amount of cosmic rays would result in severe burns or even death. These rays destroy body tissue and the blood cells in our bodies. Fortunately, only a small portion of these rays reach us here on earth. Many of these rays are trapped thousands of miles above the earth; only a minute amount come through to us. However, as we go out into space we are exposed to this increased amount of cosmic rays, or cosmic radiation, as scientists call it. Satellites have sent back information that the earth is surrounded by a huge swarm of high-speed, electrically charged atomic particles, beginning about 500 miles above the equator and extending about 40,000 miles out into space. These particles form a huge doughnut-shaped belt, with the earth at the center of the "doughnut." This belt was named after its discoverer, Dr. James Van Allen.

WHAT OTHER RADIATION IS DANGEROUS TO MAN IN SPACE?

Two other rays given off by the sun have created problems for the space traveler. The invisible gamma rays and the dangerous ultraviolet rays fill the atmosphere above the earth. Like the cosmic rays, only a small portion of these ever reach the earth. The gamma rays can be stopped in space by the metal surface of a spaceship. The ultraviolet rays, which cause severe burns, can be stopped by a special type of glass. Thus, it is possible for the spaceman to be protected from these rays. He

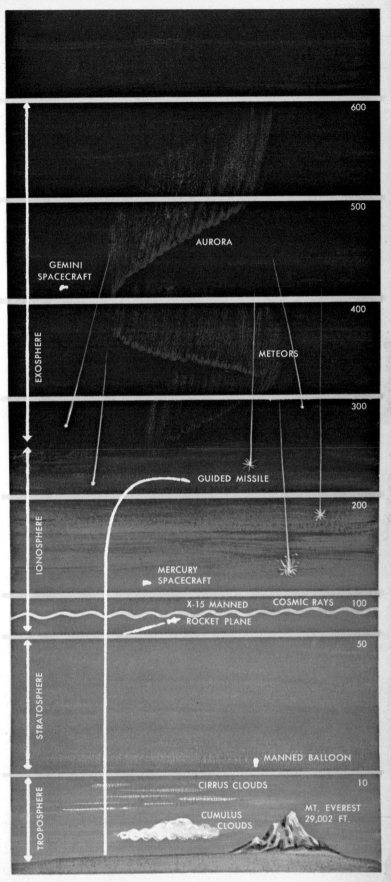

The air between earth and outer space is the atmosphere.

can be protected from all but the most violent cosmic rays by the walls of the spaceship. Further protection comes through scientific monitoring of the rays. This provides the spaceman with warning of possible danger.

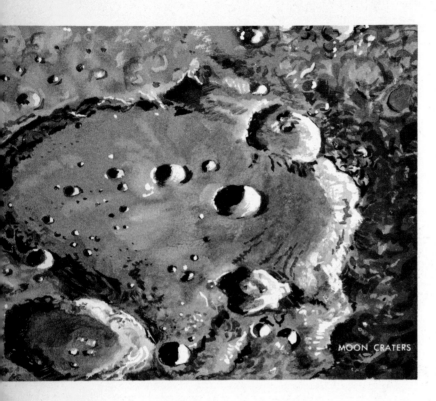

MOON CRATERS

WHAT IS THE
MOON LIKE?

Our nearest neighbor in the solar system, the moon at its *perigee* (PER-i-gee), or nearest point to the earth, is 221,463 miles. At its *apogee* (AP-o-gee), or farthest point away from the earth, it is 252,712 miles away. Even with a small telescope, it is possible to see many details of the moon's surface on a clear night. Its rotation on its axis and its revolution about the earth are synchronized so that only one side of the moon faces the earth at all times.

The surface of the moon which we see has four distinct characteristics. First, there are the lofty mountains. The Leibnitz and Doerfel Mountains in the southern part of the moon exceed 30,000 feet. Second, there are the broad dark plains or "seas" of the moon, which are visible with the naked eye. The third and most outstanding feature of the moon are the craters. They are very deep and very wide and can be found almost everywhere on the surface. The Clavius crater, for example, is 17,000 feet deep and 145 miles in diameter. Finally, there are the rills.

These are long, very deep crevices that are sometimes a mile or more wide at the top.

ARE THE MOON'S SEAS
REALLY OCEANS OF WATER?

The great level plain areas of the moon are called "seas." The earliest astronomers, gazing at the moon with their primitive telescopes, did not know that the moon was a lifeless, waterless body, and reasoned that parts of its surface must be covered by water like the seas on earth. We know now that the "seas" are dust-covered deserts, but they have been allowed to keep their original designations as "seas."

The winds and waters of earth are constantly at work to change the earth's surface and erase the marks of its geologic history. But the moon is without the erosive effects of wind and water. Thus, it is almost certain that every scar inflicted on the moon's surface in the past two or three billion years remains exactly as it was when it was first made. Scientists have not observed any new craters of appreciable size that have been created on the moon since the invention of the telescope. From this we might conclude that the meteoric bombardment of the moon — especially by giant meteors — has not been as great in the last few hundred or few thousand years as it was in the distant past.

HOW BIG IS THE MOON?

The moon is 2,160 miles in diameter, roughly one-quarter the diameter of the earth. In relation to the width of the United States, this means that a line drawn through the axis of the moon would extend from New York to Salt Lake City, Utah. The moon's mass (roughly its weight) is 1/81st that of earth's. Since the gravitational attraction of a body depends upon its mass, scientists have determined that the pull of gravity on the moon's surface is just one-sixth of that on earth. This means that if you normally weigh 150 pounds, your weight on the moon would be only 25 pounds. If you can jump three feet into the air on earth, you could jump 18 feet on the moon. To use another example, if you can lift 100 pounds on earth, you could lift 600 pounds on the moon. Thus, when future explorers reach the moon, they will have little difficulty in moving and lifting heavy pieces of machinery and equipment that they could not even budge on earth.

WHAT ARE THE PHASES OF THE MOON?

Like the earth, the moon creates no light of its own. The moonlight we see on a clear night is only a reflection of sunlight. For this reason, the moon seems to assume different shapes at different times of the lunar month as it orbits the earth. These are called the *phases* of the moon.

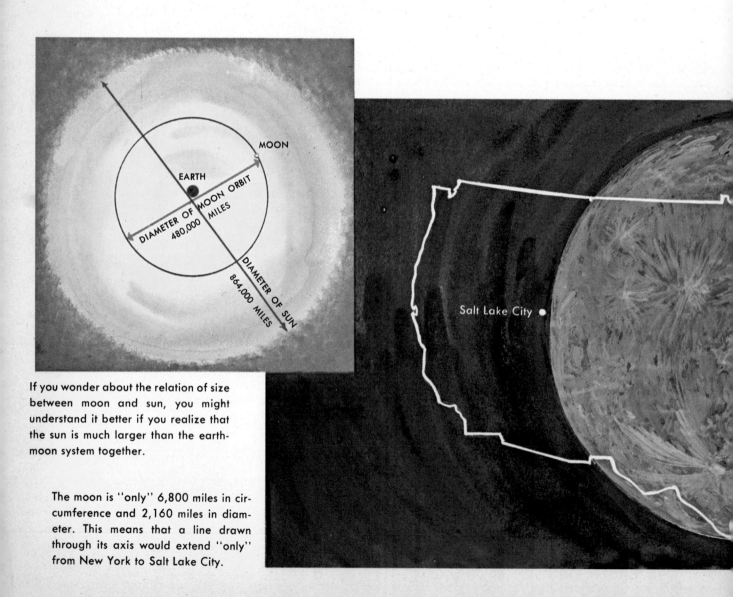

If you wonder about the relation of size between moon and sun, you might understand it better if you realize that the sun is much larger than the earth-moon system together.

The moon is "only" 6,800 miles in circumference and 2,160 miles in diameter. This means that a line drawn through its axis would extend "only" from New York to Salt Lake City.

When, in its journey around the earth, the moon comes into a direct line with the sun, we cannot see it at all. This is called the "new" moon. Twenty-four hours later, a small part of it reflects the sunlight as a thin crescent. This is commonly known as a "sickle" moon. After a week, the crescent enlarges to become a "quarter" moon. And in another week, the entire ball of the moon, or the "full" moon, is exposed to our view. The moon's phase then gradually recedes into the third quarter, into a crescent again, and finally into the new moon to complete once more its monthly circuit.

If you were an explorer standing on the moon and looking at the earth, you would see the same effects. The earth would shine in the reflected light of the sun, and you could properly call it "earthlight." At various phases of the earth's passage overhead, you would see "full" earth, "quarter" earth, and "crescent" earth. And, of course, at "new" earth, you could not see it at all. The astronauts have already experienced the thrill of looking at their home planet and taking pictures of it. At that distance, the earth appears as a large bluish white marble.

New York

HOW WAS THE MOON FORMED?

There have been a great many scientific theories about the origin of the moon. Of these, only the three most likely will be discussed here. The first holds that the moon is a thrown-off portion of the earth itself. When the earth was new and in a semi-liquid form, its rapid revolution around the sun caused it to assume the shape of a lop-sided dumbbell. The smaller part of the dumbbell broke away and became the moon. A corollary to this theory is that after the earth had begun to solidify, a huge chunk of it was torn loose from what is now the basin of the Pacific Ocean.

Other scientists believe that the moon is actually older than the earth. They contend that the moon is a relic of an earlier stage of the solar system than that during which the earth was formed. Toward the end of the earth's formation, it caught the moon in the force of its gravity and captured the moon as a permanent satellite.

Most scientists today, however, accept the theory that the moon and the earth were formed at the same time and of the same basic materials. They think that several billion years ago our solar system was nothing but a cloud of cold dust particles whirling aimlessly through the nothingness of deep space. Then, in response to the laws of gravity, these particles gradually came together to form a huge, spinning disk. As it spun, the disk separated into rings. The nucleus of the disk became the sun, and the particles in the outer rings became the planets. When both earth and moon had been formed, the moon, being much the smaller, was captured by the stronger gravity of the earth.

HOW ARE SOME OF THE MOON'S FEATURES NAMED?

The sea areas, first observed by the earliest astronomers like Galileo, were given Latin names: *Oceanus Procellarum* (Ocean of Storms), *Mare Imbrium* (Sea of Rains), *Mare Humorum* (Sea of Moisture), *Mare Nubium* (Sea of Clouds), *Mare Vaporum* (Sea of Vapors), *Mare Tranquillitatis* (Sea of Tranquillity), *Mare Foecunditatis* (Sea of Fertility), *Lacus Somniorum* (Sea of Dreams), and many others.

Most of the important mountain ranges were named for mountains on earth: Alps, Apennines, Caucasian, Jura, Carpathian, Pyrenees. Others, such as Leibnitz and Doerfel, were named for famous astronomers.

The craters also took their names from great scientists and philosophers, both ancient and modern: Plato, Copernicus, Euclid, Archimedes, Faraday, Cavendish, Ross, Pickering, Lee, Newton, and scores of others.

When the Russians made the first charts of the moon's "far side," they named the new features which they discovered: Moscow Sea, Soviet Mountains, and Tsiolkovsky, Lomonosov, and Tsu C'hung-Chin craters.

WHAT ARE THE HARVEST MOON AND HUNTER'S MOON?

The full moon which is nearest in date to the autumnal equinox (September 23) is known as the "harvest moon." At this time, the moon rises early in the evening for three nights in succession, and is entirely or nearly full on each of the nights. Thus the light of the moon lengthens the natural period of twilight, and allows farmers extra hours of working time in which to harvest their crops before the fall frosts set in. The "hunter's moon" follows the harvest moon, one month later, and is very similar to it. It is so called because the hunting season follows the gathering in of the crops.

WHAT DID PRIMITIVE MEN BELIEVE ABOUT THE MOON?

Because the moon is the nearest heavenly body to the earth, and because it appears at different times of the month in several varied forms, a great many myths and superstitions have grown up about it. Since long before the first history books were written, people believed that the full moon caused insanity. In fact, the word "lunacy" comes from the Latin word "luna" meaning moon. It was believed that if the full moon shone on a person while he was sleeping, that person would go mad. Another old superstition said that moonlight could cause blindness. But since moonlight is nothing more than reflected sunlight, the sun should cause a great deal more madness and blindness than the moon.

The moon has always figured prominently in both ancient and modern religion. It was worshipped as a goddess by the Greeks and Romans, as well as native tribes in Asia, Africa, Australia, and North and South America. Today, the phases of the moon play an important part in the celebration of both Christian and Jewish Holy Days. The Christian festival of Easter always takes place on the first Sunday after the first full moon after the vernal equinox. One of the important festivals in the Jewish faith, Passover, always falls on the first full moon of the spring, from the 14th to the 21st day of the Hebrew month Nisan.

LOW TIDE

HIGH TIDE

There is a high tide and a low tide about every six hours. In other words, during approximately every 24 hours, at any point on the shore, there are two high tides and two low tides.

HOW DOES THE MOON AFFECT THE OCEANS OF THE EARTH?

If you have ever been to the seashore, you must have observed the daily ebb and flow of the tides. At certain times during the day, the level of the water rises sometimes as much as ten or twenty feet. A few hours later the tide has receded, leaving behind it a long stretch of empty beach. These tidal flows are caused mainly by the gravitational pull of the moon, and to a lesser degree, of the sun.

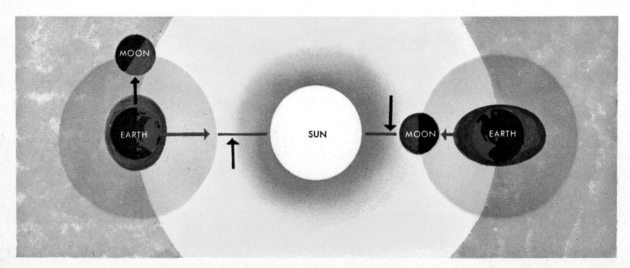

When the moon and the sun line up on the same side of the earth, or when the sun and the moon are in line, but on opposite sides of the earth, the combined gravitational pull creates unusually high or *spring tides*. When sun and moon are at right angles, the gravitational pull of each works against the other and unusually low or *neap tides* result.

28

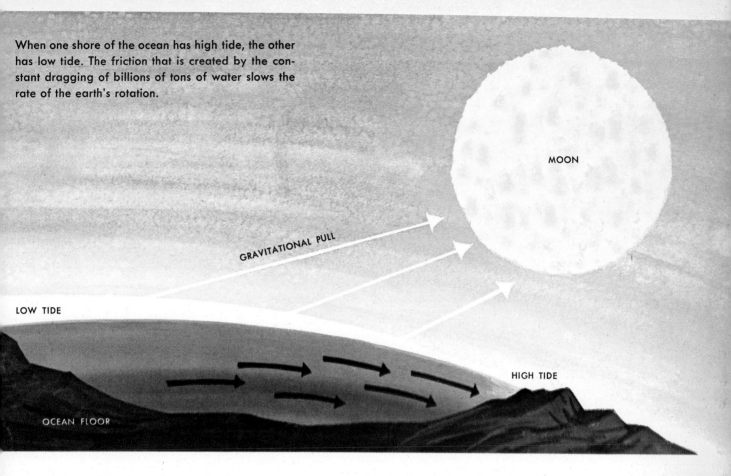

When one shore of the ocean has high tide, the other has low tide. The friction that is created by the constant dragging of billions of tons of water slows the rate of the earth's rotation.

MOON

GRAVITATIONAL PULL

LOW TIDE

HIGH TIDE

OCEAN FLOOR

During the periods of new moon and full moon, the earth, the sun, and the moon are in a straight line. Thus, the moon and sun work together to cause extremely high tides, known as "spring" tides. When the moon is in its first and third quarters, it is at right angles to the sun in relation to the earth. At these times, the moon and sun are pulling against each other, resulting in lower tides, called "neap" tides. As billions of tons of sea water are constantly being dragged back and forth across the ocean floors, the friction they create acts as a brake on the rate of the earth's rotation. And as the earth's rotation slows, the days lengthen. The result is that our days are getting about one second longer every 100,000 years.

WHAT IS AN ECLIPSE OF THE MOON?

When the full moon moves into the deep shadow of the earth and seems to disappear, we call it the *eclipse* of the moon. There are usually one or two such lunar eclipses that are visible in the United States each

A lunar eclipse occurs when the moon passes through the earth's shadow. Usually in a lunar eclipse, the moon appears darkened to a deep copper red.

year, and almost everybody has observed at least one in his lifetime. Most of us enjoy watching the spectacle of the moon being apparently swallowed up by the earth's shadow.

The earth orbits around the sun in a level plane. For example, if we suppose that the sun is in the center of a dining-room table, then the earth moves around it on the same level as the table's top. On the other hand, as the moon goes around the earth its path is tilted about five degrees. That is why we do not have an eclipse during each full moon. The earth, of course, always casts a shadow which extends nearly 859,000 miles into space, but the moon ordinarily passes above or below it. However, when the moon is in the same plane as the earth during full moon, the earth's shadow blots out the moon and an eclipse occurs.

WHAT IS AN ECLIPSE OF THE SUN?

An eclipse of the sun takes place during the new moon when the moon is between the earth and the sun. The shadow cast by the moon varies in length from 228,000 to 236,000 miles. For this reason, most of the times

A solar eclipse occurs when the moon passes between the earth and the sun, blocking view of the sun from a section of the earth.

when the moon is in the right position for a solar eclipse, the moon's shadow does not reach the earth. On the other hand, when new moon occurs during perigee (when the moon is at the lowest point in its orbit), the moon's shadow extends several thousand miles beyond the earth. On such occasions, the shadow cast by the moon onto earth may cover an area of some 475 sq. miles.

It is for these reasons that eclipses of the sun are rare and fleeting events. They last for only a few minutes, and take place at many different points over the earth's surface. If, for example, astronomers know that a solar eclipse is scheduled to occur at Kano, in Africa, on a certain date, they will spend many many months setting up their equipment at that location in order to take photographs of the phenomenon.

If you are ever lucky enough to see a total solar eclipse, you will discover that it is an awe-inspiring sight. As the moon approaches the sun, the skies begin to darken as they do at normal twilight. On the farms, chickens go to roost, thinking that it is nightfall. When the moon completely obscures the sun's flaming ball, the sky becomes almost as dark as a moonless night. Then, in a few minutes, the moon passes across the sun and disappears from view, and the day becomes bright again.

The air on earth, when exposed to the sun, evens out the temperature between sunny and shaded places. But the lack of atmosphere on the moon makes the sunlit spots "boiling hot" and the shadows "freezing cold," with nothing in between.

WHAT ARE DAYS AND NIGHTS LIKE ON THE MOON?

The earth rotates on its axis once every 24 hours. Thus, its average day and night are each of 12 hours duration. The moon orbits around the earth once every 27⅓ days, and in this same period it turns only once on its axis. Thus, the lunar "day" is equal to about 14 earth days, and the lunar "night" is of the same duration. Of course, one side of the moon is *always* illuminated by the sun — just as is one side of the earth. Thus, when it is "night" in one moon-hemisphere, it is "day" in the other.

During the "day," when the surface of the moon is fully exposed to the sun's rays, the temperature of its surface is about 220 degrees F. This is slightly higher than the boiling point of water. At "night" on the moon, the temperature plunges to about 250° F. below zero. But since the moon has no atmosphere to absorb and transfer heat, the dark shadow cast by an overhanging rock is as cold during the "day" as it would be at "night." Thus, if you were standing on the moon with your right foot in the full sunlight, and your left foot in deep shadow, then your right foot would be exposed to 220 degree heat and your left foot to 250-below-zero cold.

WHAT IS THE PLANET MERCURY LIKE?

Mercury, the nearest planet to the sun, is also the smallest. It is only slightly larger than our moon — 3,100 miles in diameter as compared with our moon's 2,160 miles. Because of its small size, there is very little gravity as compared with earth. For example, if you weigh 100 pounds on earth, you would weigh only 35 pounds on Mercury. The pull of gravity is what holds the clouds and air around the earth. On Mercury, however, there is no atmosphere because the gravity is so low. Thus, there are no clouds, no rain, no water on that planet.

Mercury completes its orbit around the sun, or makes one full trip in its ellipse, in only 88 earth days. As it takes the planet exactly the same

The hot sun shines down continually on one side of Mercury; here the heat is so intense that lead would boil.

length of time to rotate upon its axis, Mercury always keeps one side facing the sun. Here the temperature reaches almost 800° F., which is hot enough to make lead melt and boil. On Mercury's other side, where the sun never shines, the temperature drops to —460° F. At this very low temperature, it is so cold that oxygen (which we need for breathing) and nitrogen (which we have in our air) would be frozen solid. The intense heat and extreme cold, the dangerous glare from the burning sun, the lack of water and the low gravity would make it most difficult to explore the surface of Mercury. Mercury is difficult to observe, because it is never very far above the horizon at night. Astronomers observe it in the daytime, using special screens.

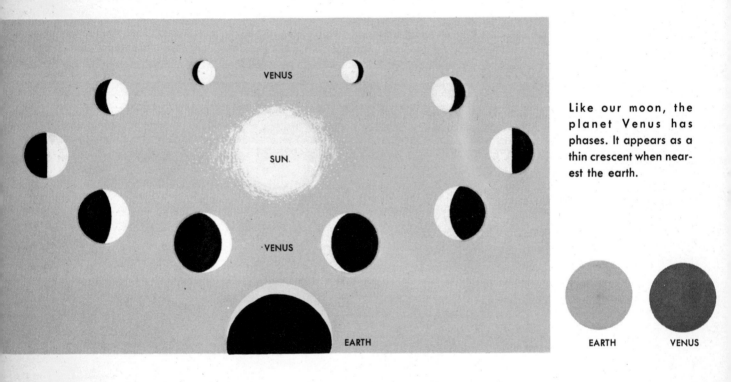

Like our moon, the planet Venus has phases. It appears as a thin crescent when nearest the earth.

EARTH   VENUS

IS VENUS LIKE THE EARTH?

Venus, about the same size as the earth, and often called "our sister planet," is also our nearest neighbor in space. At its nearest point, Venus is 26 million miles from earth. It is the brightest of all planets because of the reflection of the sun from its massive clouds. No one has ever seen the surface of Venus — even with the most powerful telescope — since the planet is always completely covered with thick white layers of clouds. These clouds are not like those we have on earth, which are composed of water vapor, ice crystals and some dust. The clouds of Venus, according to astronomers, consist of large amounts of dust, ice crystals, carbon and poisonous formaldehyde. The Venus clouds do not change their shape, and this has led scientists to conclude that there are no great oceans and land masses or continents on Venus as there are on earth. If there were large oceans and big land areas, air currents would be formed similar to those we find on earth; and if air currents were present, they would penetrate the cloud cover and cause them to move about.

WHAT WOULD LIFE BE LIKE ON VENUS?

Venus was at one time considered to be a more likely home than Mars for earthlings, but revelations by way of space probes, radar and radio astronomy are not encouraging in this respect. The average surface temperature is indicated at a rather uncomfortable 800° Fahrenheit! Then, too, there is no water on the surface; the atmosphere is deadly; and the pressure of 294 pounds per square inch is tremendous.

The planet rotates in a direction opposite to its spin around the sun once every 243 earth-days.

WHAT IS MARS LIKE?

Mars is about half the size of earth and is half again as far from the sun than the earth is. Mars rotates at about the same speed as the earth. Its day is 24 hours and 37.4 minutes of earth time. Its year, however, is about twice as long as ours, or 686.7 earth days. Because it is some 50 million miles farther from the sun than the earth, Mars receives less than half the light and heat from the sun than we do. Its temperature could be tolerated by a spaceman, since it is not too different from that on earth. Around the center of Mars, similar to the equator of earth, the daytime temperature rises to about 85° F., and at night, it drops to somewhat below freezing. At its polar regions, the temperature of Mars is slightly above freezing in the daytime, but it goes as low as $-130°$ F. at night.

Because it is smaller than earth, its gravity is lower. In fact, the gravity pull on Mars is only slightly greater than that on Mercury. Another difference is its atmosphere. While it contains water vapor and carbon dioxide, there is no trace of pure oxygen gas as there is in the earth's atmosphere.

The Martian landscape has fascinated men for centuries. Polar ice caps are visible during the winter season on Mars. During the summer, the ice caps appear to melt and the white surface of the ice disappears. In place of it we find a large green-looking area. Recent explorations of Mars with radio telescopes indicate that these polar caps are not like those on earth. Whereas the earth's polar caps are hundreds of feet thick, the Martian ice caps are about one-twenty-fifth of an inch thick.

Mars through a telescope

The ice cap over the pole of Mars shrinks and grows with the seasons.

IS THERE ANY FORM OF LIFE ON MARS?

The question of why the surface appears green has long puzzled scientists. How could life exist without oxygen in the air to breathe? This has been answered partially by plants we have on earth, lichens. These small plants produce their own oxygen in the daylight and use it at night instead of drawing it from the atmosphere. In addition to the polar caps, astronomers have observed large bright areas, reddish in color, which they thought to be deserts, and large dark areas, which they believed to be oceans. Today, scientists think that the dark areas are a form of plant life similar to that which is visible at the polar regions during the summer. Scientists also believe that the bright areas are mineral or rock surfaces.

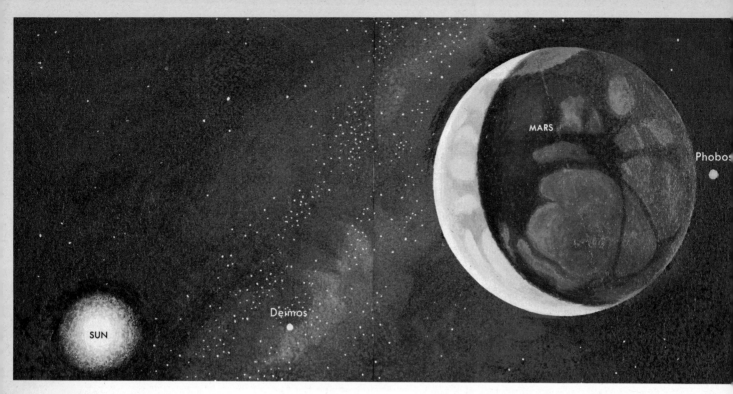

MARS

Phobos

Deimos

SUN

Mars and its moons, Phobos and Deimos.

One of the most important reasons why many people believed that intelligent life existed on Mars is the presence of what seemed to be *canals*. Many people believed that some reasoning being, like man, lived on Mars and built the canals in order to irrigate the lands. The canals are the same color as the areas thought to be oceans. Now with our use of high-powered telescopes and radio telescopes, we realize that the canals are not so narrow or so regular as was once believed. Instead, many astronomers now feel that the canals are nothing more than bands of plant life that cover the surface of the planet. While we accept the possibility that elementary plant life exists on Mars, we have no proof that intelligent life, such as man, also exists there. Mars would not be too unfriendly to the spaceman. It is far more inviting than the moon, for there are some indications that Mars is a living world rather than a dead one.

WHAT IS JUPITER LIKE?

Jupiter, the largest of all the planets, has the shortest "day" as measured by earth time — 9 hours and 55 minutes. It shines brightly in the sky because it is so large, and it is about eleven times greater in size than the earth. There are twelve moons that orbit around Jupiter in an ellipitical pattern, just as the planets do around the sun. Four of the moons are as large as, or larger than, our own moon, which is 2,160 miles in diameter. The other eight moons of Jupiter vary in size from about 15 to 100 miles in diameter.

Several large gaseous layers of clouds surround the surface of Jupiter. Some are composed of poisonous ammonia and methane gases, and others consist of hydrogen and helium gases, like those of the sun. Within one of these large cloud layers is a giant red area — "the red spot of Jupiter," as astronomers call it. This red spot is somewhat larger than the earth and it was first seen in 1875. We do not know what makes it red, but we have noticed that is has become fainter and fainter every year. Some day it may disappear entirely, or maybe a spaceship will reach it to discover why it is red. Circling the sun at a distance more than five times the distance from the sun to the earth, Jupiter receives very little light or heat from the sun. Its surface is believed to be a thick mass of ice that never melts. The surface temperature is about −215° F., and it never rises much above that extremely cold level.

The clouds of Jupiter show changing patterns.

DO WE KNOW WHAT'S INSIDE JUPITER?

For many years, Jupiter has been called a "gas giant," for it was impossible to determine whether or not it was really solid below the ice. In recent years, using radio telescopes, astronomers have found that the inner core of Jupiter is composed of hot molten material. How can the outside covering be solid ice when the inside is very hot? Wouldn't the heat melt the ice? But astronomers are sure of the ice covering and the hot molten material inside. What they do not know is what is in between. Some believe

that there is an insulating material separating the hot material inside from the ice outside. Others believe that there is a layer of water between the two. Perhaps in the future you may learn the answer after a spaceman has explored Jupiter. Because of its tremendous size, the gravity pull of the planet Jupiter is 2.64 times greater than that on earth. This means that a spaceman who weighed 200 pounds on earth would weigh 528 pounds on Jupiter. It also means that it would require much more power to blast off in a spaceship from Jupiter than it does from earth.

WHAT HAVE WE LEARNED ABOUT SATURN?

Saturn is similar to Jupiter in many ways. It, too, consists of a molten core that is surrounded by an ice cover thousands of miles thick. It also has an atmosphere filled with deadly methane and ammonia gases. However, this atmosphere is much more stable than Jupiter's; that is, it is more like own own sky on a calm, clear day as compared with our sky during a violent, windy thunderstorm. Only slightly smaller than its sister "gas giant" Saturn is almost twice as far as Jupiter is from the sun. Little of the sun's heat or light reaches the surface of Saturn. The surface temperature of the planet is believed to be about —240° F. Like Jupiter, Saturn rotates quickly. Its day is equal to 10 hours and 12 minutes of earth time. Its year, or the length of one complete revolution around the sun, is about 29½ earth years.

The rings of Saturn, visible only through a telescope, appear at different angles each year. When they are tilted toward earth, Saturn's brightness increases.

EARTH   SATURN

WHAT ARE THE STRANGE FEATURES OF SATURN?

First, it has ten moons, the largest of which, Titan, is about the size of Mercury. But unlike the planet Mercury, Titan has a very small atmosphere. Furthermore, one of the moons of Saturn revolves from east to west, or clockwise, around the planet, while the other nine moons revolve in the normal solar system direction, counterclockwise. Why this moon behaves in this manner, no one knows. It is one of the mysteries of astronomy and space.

The second strange feature about this planet is its rings. Imagine a grapefruit cut in half; one part is placed outside down on a very large plate and the other side is set against the bottom of the plate directly below the top half. This is the way the rings appear around Saturn. Saturn's rings which are much brighter than the planet itself, are composed of millions of small solid particles and ice crystals. The rings around the center of Saturn start at about 7,000 miles from the surface. There are several distinct rings and the farthest one away from the planet measures about 10 thousand miles in diameter. The whole ring system measures 170 thousand miles in diameter. Astronomers had believed that these rings were about 50 miles thick, but recent studies have put the thickness at only 10 miles. The uncertainties about the planet and its great distance from the earth mean that no spaceship will reach Saturn until we have progressed far beyond our current technological levels in space travels.

WHAT IS URANUS LIKE?

When first seen by astronomers in 1690, Uranus was thought to be a star. It was not until 1781 that Sir William Herschel of England discovered that Uranus was a planet that revolved about our sun just as the earth does.

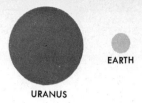

URANUS EARTH

Uranus is twice as far as Saturn is from the sun or twenty times that of the earth from the sun. Unlike all the other planets, Uranus rotates on an imaginary axis that almost points directly at the sun. It would be much the same as if our earth were turned so that the North Pole would be almost pointing at the sun. In rotating on this axis the north pole of Uranus faces the sun for almost twenty years. Then as the planet shifts, the rays of the sun move over the equator and shine over the south pole of Uranus for about twenty years. Because of its great distance from the sun, little heat reaches that planet. The surface temperature is believed to be about −300° F.

Although Uranus is four times larger than the earth, it is not as dense or as heavy as the earth. Its surface gravity is slightly less than the gravity on earth. In addition, its atmosphere, or the gases surrounding the planet, are poisonous ammonia and methane. After Uranus was discovered, astronomers were puzzled by its orbit around the sun. They knew that all heavenly bodies have a gravitational attraction or pull. Both the French astronomer Urbain Leverrier and the Englishman John C. Adams decided that there must be another planet beyond Uranus that was attracting it with its gravitational pull. Only in that way could the orbit of Uranus be explained.

Uranus rotates strangely on its axis with the sun shining on the planet's north pole for 20 years. The planet then turns and its south pole faces the sun for 20 years.

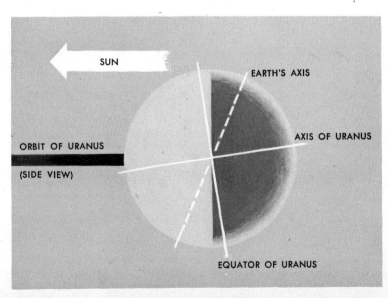

SUN

EARTH'S AXIS

AXIS OF URANUS

ORBIT OF URANUS

(SIDE VIEW)

EQUATOR OF URANUS

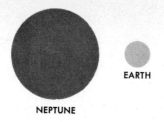

NEPTUNE   EARTH

WHAT WAS THE
"MYSTERY" PLANET?

In 1848, the German astronomer Johann Galle located the new planet, Neptune, with his telescope exactly where Urbain Leverrier had predicted it would be. Neptune is the outermost of the four "gas giants" and is more than three times larger than the earth. Its surface gravity is almost one-and-a-half times greater than on earth — and is greater than any planet's surface gravity except Jupiter's. Like its sister "gas giants," it is covered with ammonia and methane gas clouds over an icy surface. Astronomers believe that the temperature on Neptune's surface is about −330° F.

Neptune, as it would be seen from one of its moons.

In some ways, Neptune and Uranus are more similar than the earth and Venus. The main difference between these two planets is that Neptune is somewhat colder and slightly smaller. It also appears bluish, while Uranus has a greenish hue when observed with a telescope. Little is known about the surface of either of these two distant planets, and we can only guess that the surface would be somewhat the same as that on Jupiter or Saturn.

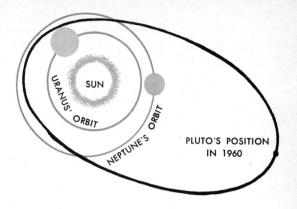

Both Pluto and Neptune revolve about the sun, but their orbits overlap and the planets cross each other twice in one complete revolution. A collision is possible, but it is thought unlikely since the nearest the two planets get to each other is 24 million miles.

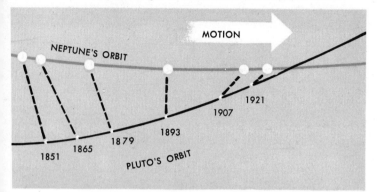

MOTION

NEPTUNE'S ORBIT

1921
1907
1893
1879
1865
1851
PLUTO'S ORBIT

After Neptune was discovered, astronomers found that they still could not fully explain the orbit of Uranus. There had to be another heavenly body which was exerting a gravitational pull on Uranus so that it followed its strange orbit around the sun. A search was begun to find the missing planet. The letter X, used by mathematicians to signify an unknown quantity, was used as the name of the missing planet during the search.

WHY WAS "PLANET X" CALLED PLUTO?

In 1900, the American astronomer Percival Lowell started on his long search for Planet X. He directed much of the search and, finally, in 1930, the missing planet was found by Clyde Tombaugh. This planet was labeled "PL" for Percival Lowell and was called Pluto. Pluto is amazing in many ways. It is more than 3½ billion miles from our sun. Its year, or one revolution around the sun, takes more than 248 earth years. The planet is somewhat larger than Mercury, and its interior is more like the earth's than its neighboring "gas giants." In studying Pluto, astronomers found that its orbit cut across Neptune's. Will they ever collide? Many years were spent to answer this question. It was found that the difference in speed at which these two planets revolve about the sun has prevented them from colliding thus far.

Astronomers measure the distance to a nearer star by observing it from opposite points in the earth's orbit around the sun. By noting the change in the star's apparent position from the two points, they can measure the angles of the triangle shown. Since they know the distance AB, they can calculate the distance to the star by geometry, a branch of mathematics.

HOW DO ASTRONOMERS MEASURE DISTANCE?

Because of the very large distances they must measure in space, astronomers have developed special units of measure. In this way they can avoid using all those zeros, such as we encounter in measuring the distance of Pluto to the sun —3,500,000,000 miles. One of the basic astronomical units is a *light-year*. Light travels at the speed of 186,000 miles per second. In one day a ray of light travels over 16,000,000,000 miles. In one year it travels 5,880,000,000,000 miles. To the astronomer, this is one light-year. So instead of writing this number with all the zeros, the astronomer merely writes "one light-year."

The convenience of the light-year unit of measure is readily seen when we start talking about distances to the stars. You have looked up into the sky at night and seen the stars. But what is a star? A star is a heavenly body that shines by its own light. That means it must be very hot to give off heat and light, just like our sun. Actually, our sun is a star; it is the nearest star to us — 93 million miles away.

Aside from our sun, how far is the nearest star? That star, called Proxima Centauri, is almost 25 trillion miles away. To the astronomer this is 4¼ light-years. The next nearest star is Alpha Centauri, and it is 500 billion miles farther away than Proxima Centauri. Alpha Centauri is in the constellation, or star group, known as *Centaurus,* and it has the same brightness as our sun. However, it is so far away that it appears as a mere dot in our sky.

HOW WERE

STARS FORMED?

One theory is that stars are formed out of the clouds of atoms, mostly hydrogen, that are scattered through space. When enough atoms collect, the gravity between them pulls them closer and closer together until they begin to form a ball. As they continue to be squeezed together, they bump against each other so hard that they produce more and more heat, until finally they start the atomic chain reaction that leads them to blaze like the sun. Finally,

ANDROMEDA

MILKY WAY

SOLAR SYSTEM

as it condenses more and more, the star becomes as compact and hot as the white dwarfs. There is probably a limit to how far this process can go, since the more compressed the atoms are the more active they become from the heat that their collisions generate. Finally there is an explosion and the atoms are again scattered into clouds, from which the process can start all over again. Explosions have been seen that would appear to be just such an end to a star.

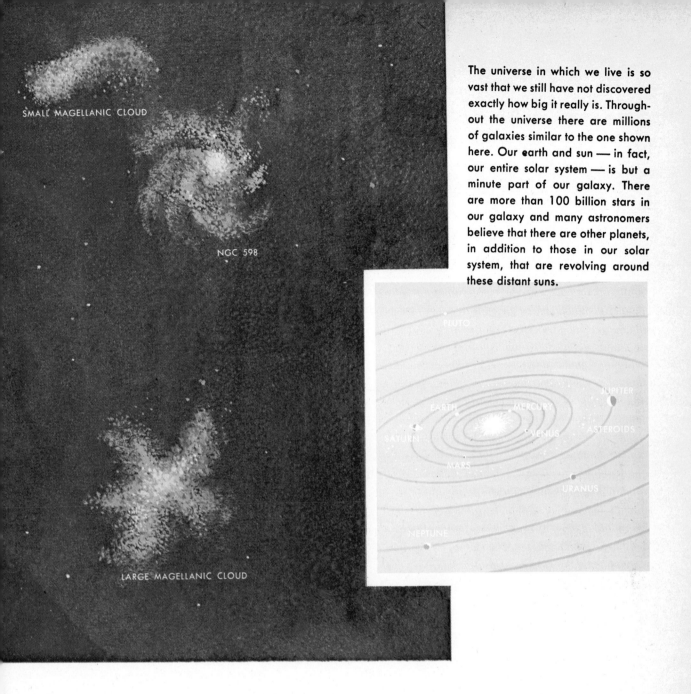

SMALL MAGELLANIC CLOUD

NGC 598

LARGE MAGELLANIC CLOUD

PLUTO

JUPITER

EARTH MERCURY

SATURN VENUS ASTEROIDS

MARS

URANUS

NEPTUNE

The universe in which we live is so vast that we still have not discovered exactly how big it really is. Throughout the universe there are millions of galaxies similar to the one shown here. Our earth and sun — in fact, our entire solar system — is but a minute part of our galaxy. There are more than 100 billion stars in our galaxy and many astronomers believe that there are other planets, in addition to those in our solar system, that are revolving around these distant suns.

HOW BIG IS OUR GALAXY?

The number of stars in our galaxy has been estimated as high as 200,000,000,000. It has been shown that the number would have to be more than 30,000,000,000. The dimensions of the galaxy are somewhere between 100,000 and 200,000 light-years across, and 10,000 to 20,000 light-years thick at the middle. Our sun is located 35,000 to 50,000 light-years from the center. The whole system is in motion, with all the stars whirling around the center. Our sun would make one revolution around the center in about 250,000,000 years, and this is whirling, considering the distance!

When we look at the Milky Way on a clear, dark night, we notice that there seem to be breaks and holes in the light band. These are not holes, but black clouds of cold star material that black out the stars beyond. It is from this material that we believe new stars are eventually formed. Is this galaxy of stars all there is in the universe? Far from it! We have learned that the Milky Way island is but one of countless galaxies like it. The nearest of these, the Great Spiral in Andromeda, can occasionally be seen by the unaided eye. It appears to be almost a twin of our own. In fact, much that we have learned of our own galaxy has been from observing it.

HOW DO THE STARS MOVE?

The real motion of the stars relative to each other should not be confused with the apparent motion due to the earth's rotation. The stars' real motion seems extremely slow to us because they are so far away. Actually, they are moving at tremendous speeds. And our sun is no exception. It appears to be heading at a terrific speed toward a point in the constellation Hercules, carrying all its planets along with it. Where are the stars going? All those we can see as individual stars are moving round and round in one giant system called a galaxy.

From our position within this system we see the heart of it as a pale white band across our sky — it is the familiar Milky Way. The Milky Way, as a telescope shows, is composed of stars so close together that they give the appearance of a shining cloud. This is an inside view of our galaxy. From far enough outside, it would look like a fiery pinwheel from one view and like a disk, swollen at the center, from an edgewise view. Our solar system is located well out near the edge of the disk. When we look at the Milky Way in the sky, we are looking toward the center of the disk; consequently, we see stars one behind the other, until they merge together. In a direction away from the Milky Way in the sky, we see only the stars in our own part of the disk, so they appear more widely scattered.

WHAT DOES A STAR'S BRIGHTNESS TELL US?

Those stars that are brighter are not necessarily any bigger than the others. A star's brightness depends on three things: its size, its distance, and the kind of star it is. Some stars give off more light than others the same size. The brightest star in our sky, Sirius, is a small star that happens to be relatively close. The closest star is rather bright, but the next closest is invisible without a telescope. The stars were classified in ancient times by how bright they appeared. Ptolemy called this their magnitude. He broke the stars down into six groups, from the brightest (first magnitude) to the faintest (sixth magnitude). There are about 4,000 stars of the first six magnitudes. The term is still in use, but the measurement has been refined and extended until astronomers can speak of a magnitude of 21.3, for example.

One of the things that determines the apparent brightness of a star is the actual intensity of its light. If you watch a piece of iron being melted, you will notice that it first begins to glow a dull red, gradually grows more orange and then yellow and finally white. The colors of the stars indicate in much the same way how hot and, therefore, how bright they are. The red stars are the coolest. The yellow stars, like our sun, are moderately hot in the scale, and the white and blue-white stars are the hottest.

WHAT ELSE DOES A STAR'S COLOR MEAN?

Their colors seem to be related also to the size of stars. The biggest stars are red, the stars in the middle range of size are yellow, and the smallest stars are white and blue-white. One of the most interesting things about this range in size is that there is not a tremendous difference in the actual amount of material in the different sizes of stars. The material is more spread out in the large stars and more condensed in the small ones. Ninety per cent of the stars we know about have a mass of not less than one tenth nor more than ten times that of our sun. The range of sizes, however, extends from dwarfs hardly larger than the earth to giants that would hold the entire solar system. It seems as if the different sizes and colors of stars might represent different stages of development. That is what astronomers believe. However, they have not determined what the process is, since stars appear to fall into different groups when they are classified according to their various properties.

A nova, an exploding star.

WHAT ABOUT
OTHER GALAXIES?

Some galaxies seem to be formless. These are assumed to be galaxies in the making. Two of these smaller star clouds are very bright in the sky of the far Southern Hemisphere. They were first reported by the explorer Magellan as he rounded South America on man's first trip around the world. Consequently, they are called Magellanic clouds. Other galaxies have a simpler elliptical shape than the spirals. They are assumed to be older and more stable systems. There are also some small "globular clusters" of stars just outside our galaxy.

Even the galaxies themselves seem to be grouped into systems. Beyond our group of about fifteen galaxies there appear to be other groups. One of these groups seems to contain over 1,000 galaxies. On a single photograph made with the 200-inch reflecting telescope at Mount Palomar, more than 10,000 galaxies were detected! Having found that the planets move in a definite pattern and that the stars move in turn in a pattern in their galaxies, the question naturally arises: do the galaxies themselves move together in some stable pattern of their own? The answer is one of the most astonishing things that science has ever been faced with: the galaxies are apparently all flying away from each other at tremendous speeds and their speeds get greater the farther apart they are!

WHAT'S HAPPENING TO THE UNIVERSE?

Nobody knows, but this question has produced some of the most fantastic-sounding and yet carefully thought-out pictures of the universe that man has ever conceived. Most of the theories involve higher mathematics and Einstein's Theory of Relatively. Consequently, it is not possible to explain here how they were arrived at, but in general they take one of two views.

The first is called *evolutionary*. Scientist-philosophers who take this view believe that the universe was created in one giant explosion of one ball of energy; the galaxies created by the explosion are still hurtling outward. Mathematicians are even able to calculate that the explosion took place somewhere between five and eight billion years ago. Some thinkers who agree with this view say that the present is just one stage of a repeating process. At a certain point the process will be reversed and the universe will contract again to one ball, only to explode again. This sounds familiar from the theory we discussed of how stars are made.

The other main view of the universe is called the *steady-state* or *balanced* universe. This view holds that the universe has no beginning and no end, that it always has had and always will have about the same distribution of material.

An orbiting astronomical observatory *(OAO2)* with eleven telescopes that was launched on December 7, 1968, has provided data which would seem to substantiate the "big bang" or expanding universe theory, according to some astronomers. Orbiting the earth at an altitude of 480 miles, this 4,400-pound observatory can determine with greater precision the radiation from large stars that is not able to penetrate the earth's atmosphere.

IS THERE LIFE ANYWHERE ELSE IN THE UNIVERSE?

There are many people who believe that no intelligent, reasoning forms of life can exist in the choking atmosphere of Venus, or on the arid surfaces of Mars or, in fact, anywhere else in our solar system. Others, however, feel that life in some form may exist, but it would certainly be different from the life forms we know on earth. Thus far, there has been no definite proof to support the views of either side.

Early in 1961, scientists at the National Institute of Health in Washington, D. C. announced that they had started to grow "life" that they believed came from another world. These "bugs," as they called them, were little twisted rods about eight- to sixteen-millionths of an inch long. They found this "life" inside a meteorite that fell at Murray, Kentucky in 1950. This "life," according to the scientists, was unlike anything we have ever found on earth. Another group of scientists discovered waxy compounds inside a fragment of a meteorite that fell near Orgueil, France in 1864.

Although there are some scientists who feel these two findings are now definite proof that life does exist elsewhere in the solar system, there are many others who do not accept these "proofs" of life. They feel that the waxy compounds are too similar to those we have on earth and that the meteorite became contaminated over the years, thus producing this strange substance. They also feel that the little twisted rods of life, which the Washington scientists presented, come from high up in our own atmosphere. Not until man is able to explore space more thoroughly and travel through it in his own spaceship, will he be able to obtain a definite answer about life on other planets.

WHAT ARE THE CHANCES OF FINDING LIFE ON ANOTHER PLANET?

Human life, according to scientists, developed on this planet because of the unique combination of many factors — the earth's distance from the sun, the composition of our atmosphere, the structure of the earth's surface, the presence of certain organisms on the face of the planet. Yet, many ask, are we the only ones in the universe?

Although astronomers have never actually seen a planet outside of our solar system, they now recognize that other solar systems exist. With powerful radio telescopes, they have located these distant systems. Astronomer Harlow Shapley has estimated that there may be life in the planetary systems of one out of a million stars. Let's take this million-to-one chance that astronomer Shapley believes and see what the chances really are! Our best scientific information tells us that there are over 100 billion stars in our own galaxy, and that there are about 100 million galaxies in the universe. This means that there are some 10 quintillion (10,000,000,000,-000,000,000) stars in the universe.

HOW CAN I LEARN THE NAMES OF THE STARS AND CONSTELLATIONS?

Charts of the major constellations are printed on the last page of the book. The simple instructions on page 58 show you how to mount the charts so that they will be most useful at any place and time. When mounted, one side of the chart shows the sky as it appears looking north and the other side shows the stars to the south. The straight border of each cardboard mask represents the horizon.

The first thing necessary in learning to use the chart is, curiously enough, to put yourself back in history many centuries and imagine the universe as the ancients conceived it. Think of the sky as a hollow globe with the stars fixed to it and imagine that the globe revolves around the earth as its center.

Once we can picture the sky as a globe, we can fix positions on it by the same means that we describe positions on earth. Everyone has seen a globe map of the earth. If you look at one carefully, you will notice that there are circles drawn on its surface. Some of these circles pass through both the North and South Poles. These are called meridians. The other circles cut the meridians at right angles and go around the earth parallel to each other. These are called parallels of latitude and the one halfway between the poles is the equator. Both meridians and parallels are numbered so we can describe the location of any spot on earth by naming the meridian and the parallel that pass through it.

HOW DO THE CIRCLES

HELP FIND STARS?

We can imagine circles on the celestial sphere that correspond exactly to the same circles on earth. On your chart the circles are parallels of latitude and the straight lines are meridians. The meridians appear as straight lines because the chart is drawn as if we were looking directly at the north and south poles of the sky. If you look straight down at the North Pole of a globe map of the earth, the meridians will look like straight lines running from the pole to the equator. The outer circle of your chart, then, represents the celestial equator.

Now that you have an idea of the "geography" of the sky, you are ready to put your chart to use. When you set your chart for the date, it will show the sky as it appears about 9 P.M. (10 P.M. Daylight Time). If the hour is later, move it counterclockwise the distance of one meridian for each hour. If the time is earlier than 9 P.M., move it clockwise. This is necessary because the celestial sphere rotates. It turns completely around once every 24 hours. Therefore, in one hour it will have moved the distance between two adjoining meridians on the chart. This rotation is counterclockwise.

HOW TO MOUNT THE STAR CHARTS

1. You will need three pieces of heavy cardboard 7½ inches square. On one (cardboard A in the picture), draw a circle in the exact center, setting the compasses at 2¾ inches. Cut out this circle with a sharp blade, taking care not to damage the edge of either the circle or the remaining piece. Smooth the edges with light sandpaper, if necessary, to permit the circle to turn easily when replaced in its hole.

2. Label one of the other pieces of cardboard "North" (this is cardboard B in the picture), and the other "South" (cardboard C). In the center of each draw a circle 2½ inches in radius. Draw a line through the center and parallel to the sides of the cardboard. Now you must find the *latitude* of your home. It will determine the size of the cutouts in cardboards B and C. If you can't find it from a map, your local weather bureau can tell you the latitude of the town. Your latitude in the United States will lie somewhere between about 26 degrees and about 45 degrees. Now convert your latitude into inches for your chart by letting 10 degrees of latitude equal ¼ inch. Thus, if you live in New York City, which is about 41 degrees, your measurement will be just about 1 inch.

3. On cardboard B, labeled "North," measure off your latitude distance along the center line *down* from the center of the circle. At this point draw a line across the circle at right angles to the center line. Everything above this line within the circle is to be cut out, including the notch at the top, shown in the illustration.

4. On cardboard C, labeled " South," measure the same latitude distance *up* from the center of the circle, draw a line at right angles, and cut out the small portion shown above the line, as in the illustration.

5. *After you have read all the instructions and know clearly how to put the chart together, cut out the star charts from the last page of the book.* Paste one chart on each side of the disk cut from cardboard A, matching up the months exactly. With the disk in place in its hole, put the three pieces of cardboard together as shown, with the cutouts of B and C both at the top. Tape the edges together or glue the three pieces together at the edges. Make sure the circle turns easily. Label the horizon and celestial equator as shown.

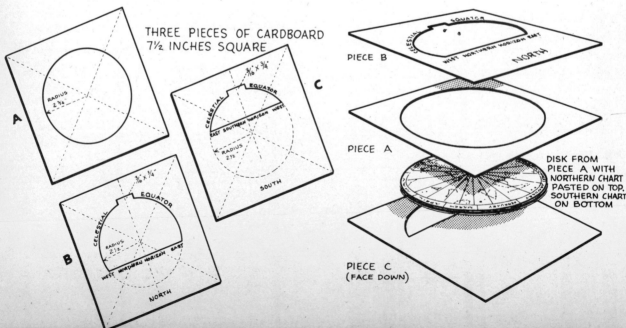

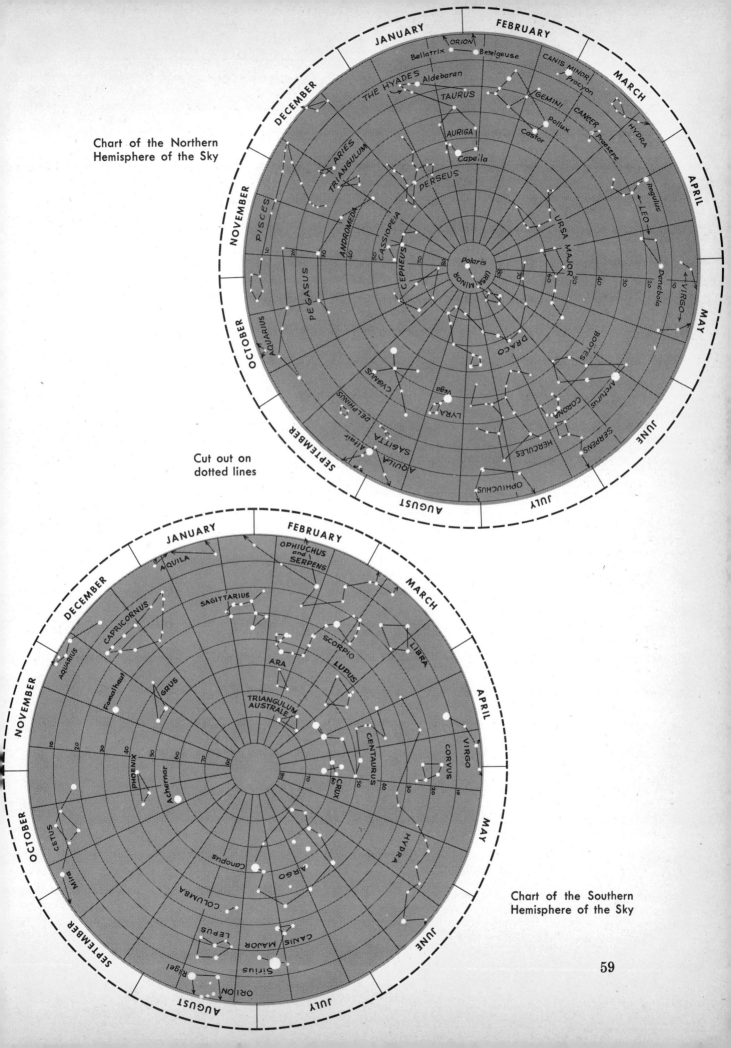

Chart of the Northern
Hemisphere of the Sky

Cut out on
dotted lines

Chart of the Southern
Hemisphere of the Sky

59

INDEX